JOURNALIST

By William David Thomas

Reading Consultant: Susan Nations, M.Ed.,
author/literacy coach/consultant in literacy development

Gareth Stevens
Publishing

Please visit our web site at **www.garethstevens.com.**
For a free catalog describing Gareth Stevens Publishing's list of high-quality books, call 1-800-542-2595 (USA) or 1-800-387-3178 (Canada).
Gareth Stevens Publishing's fax: 1-877-542-2596

Library of Congress Cataloging-in-Publication Data
Thomas, William, 1947-
   Journalist / by William David Thomas.
      p. cm. — (Cool careers : on the go)
   Includes bibliographical references and index.
     ISBN-13: 978-1-4339-0004-4   ISBN-10: 1-4339-0004-1 (lib.bdg.)
     ISBN-13: 978-1-4339-0168-3   ISBN-10: 1-4339-0168-4 (softcover)
     1. Journalism — Juvenile literature. 2. Journalism — Vocational guidance — Juvenile literature. I. Title.
   PN4776.T46   2009
   070.4—dc22   2008031733

This edition first published in 2009 by
Gareth Stevens Publishing
A Weekly Reader® Company
1 Reader's Digest Rd.
Pleasantville, NY 10570-7000 USA

Copyright © 2009 by Gareth Stevens, Inc.

Executive Managing Editor: Lisa M. Herrington
Creative Director: Lisa Donovan
Editor: Joann Jovinelly
Designer: Paula Jo Smith
Photo Researcher: Kimberly Babbitt
Publisher: Keith Garton

Picture credits: Cover and title page: David Stluka/Getty Images; p. 5 Chris Hondros/Getty Images; p. 6 Alex Wong/Getty Images; p. 7 Mark Peterson/Corbis; p. 8 Richard Hutchings/Corbis; p. 10 Bettmann/Corbis; p. 12 Erica Berger/Corbis; p. 13 Courtesy of Mark Hare; pp. 14-15 AP/CBS News, John Paul Filo; p. 16 Richard Levine/Alamy; p. 17 Mike Goldwater/Alamy; p. 18 Tom Sibley/Corbis; p. 19 Bettmann/Corbis; p. 20 Noah Graham/NBAE (via Getty Images); p. 21 AP Photo/Kevin Frayer; p. 22 Rusty Jarrett/Getty Images for NASCAR; p. 23 AP Images; p. 24 Bettmann/Corbis; p. 25 Margaret Bourke-White/Time Life Pictures/Getty Images; p. 26 Margaret Bourke-White/Life Magazine, Copyright Time, Inc./Time Life Pictures/Getty Images; p. 27 Alfred Eisenstaedt/Corbis; p. 28 Jehad Nga/Corbis

Printed in the United States of America

1 2 3 4 5 6 7 8 9 10 09 08

CONTENTS

Words in the glossary appear in **bold** type the first time they are used in the text.

CHAPTER 1

GETTING THE STORY

In June 2008, Ivan Watson rode into a war zone. He joined a line of trucks taking supplies to U.S. Marines in Afghanistan. He soon learned what was most important to them.

Dirt, Bombs, and Spiders

Watson is a **journalist** for National Public Radio (NPR). That news station is **broadcast** on the radio across the United States. Watson learned that the Marines had no showers or electricity in their camp. Their tents had dirt floors and were overrun by spiders. Bombs were going off nearby. What did the Marines want most? Mail. One Marine told Watson, "If mail's on the truck, it's the highlight of the day." That was the main idea of the story Watson wrote for NPR.

What Do Journalists Do?

Journalists write stories about people and events. Some are about politics, forest fires, or rising fuel costs. Others are about soccer games, elections, or movies. Journalists learn about situations and events and report the facts.

News reporters in war zones take notes for their stories while on the front lines.

A television reporter once said, "I'm basically a nosy person. I like asking questions." Journalists ask: *What* happened? *When* did it happen? *What* did you see? *Who* else saw it? *Why* did it happen? *How* did it happen?

Journalists get the facts and then write the story. They often do so quickly, because news is happening every minute. Once a story is written, it may be printed in a newspaper, broadcast on television, or posted on the Internet.

Where Do Journalists Work?

Many journalists travel to places where the news is happening. That might be across the street, across the country, or across an ocean. If there is an earthquake, an election, or a big football game, journalists will be there. Many **reporters** work for newspapers, magazines, or Internet sites. Broadcast journalists work at radio and TV stations. Many journalism jobs are in big cities. Small towns also have newspapers and radio stations.

Meet the Man from *Meet the Press*

In 1991, Tim Russert (1950–2008) became the host of television's oldest news show. *Meet the Press* has been on the air since 1947. As host, Russert **interviewed** presidents, members of Congress, and world leaders. He was famous for being well prepared and asking important questions. In 2008, *Time* magazine named Russert one of the 100 most important people in the world. Russert was working on the next broadcast of *Meet the Press* when he died in 2008.

In the field, reporters often take notes during public events and interviews.

Many students who are interested in journalism start by writing for their school newspapers. Later, budding reporters go on to college. Nearly every journalist has a four-year degree. College classes include writing, interviewing, and broadcasting skills. Some journalists have degrees in science, business, or law.

Could You Be a Journalist?

If you think you'd like to be a journalist, ask yourself these questions:

- Do you like to write?
- Are you interested in the events that make news?
- Do you like traveling to new places?
- Can you work fast and meet **deadlines**?
- Are you comfortable asking people questions?

If so, journalism may be the right career for you!

CHAPTER 2
PRINT AND ONLINE JOURNALISTS

The fire began at night. A news reporter rushed to the scene. Firefighters, police officers, and neighbors crowded the street. The reporter wrote down the address of the burning house. Then she began to ask questions.

Reporters have to stay cool in emergencies. They must get the facts about fires, floods, accidents, and crimes.

Every Minute Counts

The reporter talked to the people in the street. Who lived in the house? What were their names and ages? Did they all get out? The reporter also talked to the fire chief. She asked when and where the fire started. What caused it? How many firefighters were working? Were any of them injured?

At 3 A.M., the reporter went to her office. She sat down at a computer and typed quickly, but carefully. She only had a short time before the paper would be printed. She e-mailed the story to her **editor** who posted it online. Then the reporter went home and slept for a few hours. She was back in the office at 9 A.M.

The 5Ws and One H

British author Rudyard Kipling (1865–1936) was once a newspaper reporter. He wrote a poem to remind himself what should be in a good news story.

I keep six honest serving-men
(They taught me all I knew);
Their names are What and Why and When
And How and Where and Who.

Today's journalists still write stories that include the "five Ws and one H" in Kipling's poem.

The Power of the Press

Reporters don't always know where a story will take them. In 1972, Bob Woodward (left) and Carl Bernstein (right) were reporters for *The Washington Post*. They **investigated** a burglary at a Washington, D.C., office building called the Watergate. Woodward and Bernstein learned that the burglars were paid by people who worked for President Richard Nixon. They kept digging for more information. Their work helped prove that the president knew about the burglary and tried to cover it up. Woodward and Bernstein "broke" the story of Nixon's involvement in the Watergate scandal. In 1974, President Nixon resigned from office.

Blogging Away

Online journalism has grown over the last decade. Among the most important web sites are **blogs**, or web logs. People write blogs to share information or opinions. News bloggers follow the news closely and then write articles based on their opinions. In 2004, the number of blogs reached 5 million. A year later, Technorati, a company that tracks Internet activity, announced that there were more than 14 million blogs. That number doubles roughly every six months. Professional journalists write some of today's blogs. Print newspapers and magazines hire journalists to write and edit their blogs and web sites.

Information on the Go

Reporters collect information. Sometimes they read books, search through old files, or do research on the Internet. Most often, reporters interview people. To get good information, reporters must be professional. They must get people to trust them.

To meet people and get facts, reporters often have to travel. Some reporters work in other countries. They may speak other languages or work with **interpreters**. Their jobs can be dangerous. They may be reporting about wars. No matter where they are, reporters must work quickly to meet deadlines.

News anchor Neil Cavuto (in a dark suit) of the Fox Business Network meets with producers and reporters to discuss the day's stories.

Putting It All Together

There are always more news stories happening than can be printed. Editors decide which stories are the most important to print or post on the Internet. They decide how long each story will be. Typically, there are different editors for world news, local news, sports, business, and politics. Large organizations may have news teams. Each team has some reporters, a photographer, and an editor. In the smallest news organizations, one person may do all of those jobs.

On the Job: Journalist Mark Hare

Mark Hare has been a journalist for 30 years. He writes for the Democrat and Chronicle, *a daily newspaper in Rochester, New York.*

Q: Why did you become a journalist?

Hare: I loved the idea of helping people better understand their community and how it works.

Q: What jobs have you held as a journalist?

Hare: [I've been] a reporter, an **editorial** writer, and an editorial page editor. I became a **columnist** in 1997.

Q: What is the best thing about journalism as a career?

Hare: The best thing is knowing you are doing something important and useful. The people who read the paper will be better informed and better able to make good decisions.

Q: What is the worst thing?

Hare: The hours can be very long and exhausting.

Q: What is the most interesting thing you've written about?

Hare: The Rochester ice storm of March 1991, when tens of thousands of people lost power, phone service, and heat. The outage lasted for weeks, and the streets were full of downed trees. Older people had to move to shelters. We were able to report how the disaster was impacting people's lives.

Q: What would you tell young people who are thinking about a career in journalism?

Hare: Learn as much as you can about as many subjects as you can, and write every day for practice.

CHAPTER 3

BROADCAST JOURNALISTS

A television news clip shows flashing lights and the wreck of a truck. The camera moves to a man in wet clothes holding a young boy. Both are wrapped in blankets. A reporter says, "Today a father's love was stronger than a river. Thirty-two-year-old Alfredo Gomez fought the fast-moving current to rescue his 6-year-old son Michael from the Garland River."

Pictures and people's voices are powerful. They make us watch and listen. No one knows this better than broadcast journalists. They bring us the news on radio and television. It's a job that keeps reporters — and many others — on the go.

Story, Sound, and Pictures

Radio and television reporters must get facts. They interview people. They do research. Like print journalists, they follow the "five Ws and one H" rule: who, what, when, where, why, and how. When radio and television reporters go to get a story, however, they rarely go alone.

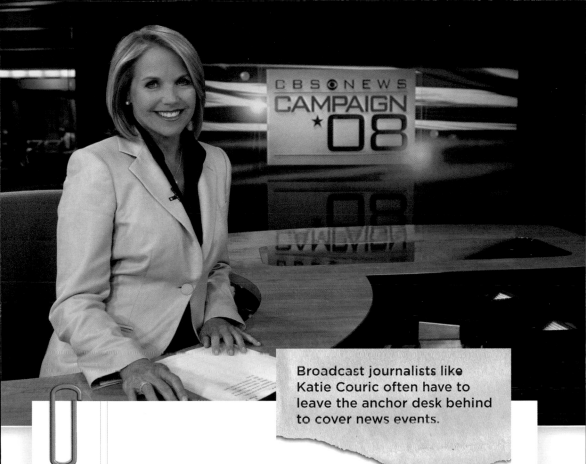

Broadcast journalists like Katie Couric often have to leave the anchor desk behind to cover news events.

Broadcast Trailblazer

In 2008, Katie Couric was the highest paid U.S. broadcast journalist, the **anchor** of *CBS Evening News*, and a reporter on *60 Minutes*. She was also among TV's most experienced reporters. Couric's early career included positions at NBC, ABC, and CNN. In the 1990s, she rose to stardom on *The Today Show*. In 2006, Couric moved to CBS. She made history as the first solo female anchor of a network nightly news program. Couric has interviewed thousands of people. She's talked with heads of state, politicians, athletes, and celebrities.

Radio reporters often travel with a sound **technician**. Someone must manage tape recorders and microphones. Listeners must hear both the reporter and the person being interviewed. Background sounds are important, too. Reporters broadcasting from a battlefield or a concert want listeners to hear what is going on.

Television reporters are usually part of a news crew. To get images and sound for their stories, TV reporters need video cameras and people to operate them. They need extra lights and sound equipment, too. News crews travel in small vans. One person on the crew usually drives the van and carries the gear.

It takes a team to broadcast the news. The reporters, camera crew, and sound and light technicians must work together.

Reporters and editors use equipment to watch and edit film and sound before the segment airs.

Crew members must work as a team. A reporter may tell a camera operator, "Be sure to get this in the shot." A camera operator may suggest a way to set up a shot. A sound technician may ask the reporter to speak more loudly or softly.

Forming the Story

After reporters bring in a story, they work with video editors. Together, they match words with pictures from the tape they've recorded. Before **digital** video, the news was shot with film cameras. Editors had to cut the film with blades and then tape it back together. Today, edits are made with digital equipment and

Breaking News

In 1980, viewers suddenly had a new way to watch cable TV news. Cable News Network (CNN) began broadcasting. It was the first 24-hour news channel. Americans could see world and national news around the clock. In 1991, CNN sent reporters into Iraq during the first Gulf War. Viewers were gripped by live broadcasts of the conflict. Today, CNN has news bureaus around the world.

computers. Sometimes a reporter makes a recording of his or her voice. This recording is called a **voice-over**. It is edited to play along with the edited video images.

Controlled by the Clock

Print journalists are limited by the number of pages in a newspaper or magazine. Broadcast journalists are limited by time. Television and radio newscasts are planned second by second.

A **producer** decides what stories will be broadcast and how long each one will last. The producer may say, "Your story is 2 minutes 45 seconds. It needs to be 2 minutes 10 seconds." The reporter and the editor must then cut 35 seconds from the edited story.

Leads and Kickers

The producer also decides the order in which stories will be broadcast. The most important story is called the **lead**. It plays first. The last story in a broadcast is often called the **kicker**. Producers usually put uplifting stories in that spot.

When the list of stories and times is ready, it goes to the anchor. This is the person who introduces or reads the stories. Some anchors are also reporters. They go out and get their own stories before going on the air.

"The Most Trusted Man in America"

Walter Cronkite (1916–) was anchor of the *CBS Evening News* from 1962 to 1981. His deep voice and bushy eyebrows became famous. Cronkite was known for being fair and honest. He was often called "the most trusted man in America." In 1968, during the Vietnam War, Cronkite said he was "more certain than ever" that the United States could not win the war. Americans believed him. Many of them stopped supporting the war.

CHAPTER 4

SPORTS JOURNALISTS

In 1989, sportscaster Al Michaels was calling Game 3 of the World Series in California. The Oakland A's were playing the San Francisco Giants. During the warm-up, viewers saw the video break up and go black. They heard Michaels say, "I'll tell you what, we're having an earth—" Then the broadcast stopped. An earthquake had hit the San Francisco Bay area.

Sports journalist Al Michaels has reported on baseball, football, basketball — and even earthquakes.

Breaking News

Moments later, viewers could only hear Michaels's voice on the air. He used a telephone to describe what was happening.

Like any good reporter, Michaels knew that viewers wanted information about the earthquake. Sports journalists are the same as other reporters: They report the news as it happens.

Some sports journalists broadcast games on radio or television. Others write stories for newspapers, magazines, and Web sites. All of them must answer the same questions as other reporters. Who won? What was the score? When did it end? Where did they play? Why did they lose?

The Beginning

Sports journalism has been around for a long time. *The Sporting News* was first printed in 1886. The small weekly newspaper became known as the "bible of Baseball." The World Series was heard on radio for the first time in 1921. Major-league baseball and pro football games were first televised in 1939.

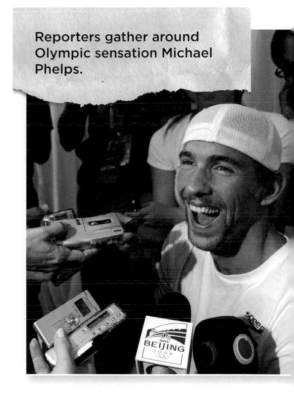

Reporters gather around Olympic sensation Michael Phelps.

Print journalism continued when television began. Red Smith (1905–1982) was a sports columnist for more than 50 years. His work appeared in 500 newspapers. *Sports Illustrated* magazine was first published in 1953. It featured longer sports stories and had exciting photographs.

Women in the Locker Room

Robin Roberts

Women are breaking barriers in sports journalism. Former Olympic swimmer Donna de Varona became one of the first female sportscasters in 1965. Leslie Visser began writing about pro football in 1976. Hannah Storm became a sports anchor for CNN in 1989. In the 1990s, Robin Roberts was a sports broadcaster for ESPN. Today, Roberts helps anchor the ABC news program *Good Morning America.*

Technology Brings Changes

Radio and television did change sports journalism, however. Because people could see and hear games, reporters began to showcase the athletes. During the 1960 Olympics, ABC showed interviews of athletes in their homes, with their families. Sports became more personal.

In 1979, the Entertainment and Sports Programming Network (ESPN) went on the air. Suddenly, sports were on television all day, every day. Besides showing games, ESPN broadcast sports news, talk shows, interviews, and editorials. ESPN also led the way in putting women in reporting and anchor roles.

Today, plenty of sports news is provided on the Internet. Much of it is written, edited, and photographed by journalists.

On the Go With Jim McKay

For more than 40 years, Jim McKay (1921–2008) hosted ABC's *Wide World of Sports*. He reported on more than 100 different sporting events for the network. McKay went to 40 countries, traveling millions of miles. He became famous for the words that opened each show: "the thrill of victory and the agony of defeat."

McKay traveled to the 1972 Olympics in Munich, Germany. During the Games, 11 athletes from Israel were kidnapped by terrorists. McKay reported on the air for 16 hours. When the Israelis were killed, McKay said sadly, "They're all gone," a line that would go down in history.

CHAPTER 5

PHOTOJOURNALISTS

In 1946, photojournalist Margaret Bourke-White traveled to India. It was a violent time in South Asia. Civil war had broken out in India. The country was on the verge of splitting into two nations—India and Pakistan. Bourke-White photographed spiritual and political leader Mahatma Gandhi. Just hours later, Gandhi was killed by a political protester. Bourke-White was the last photojournalist to see him alive. Her photos were shown around the world.

Margaret Bourke-White (1904–1971) became the first female photojournalist for *Life* magazine.

Up Close

Photographers often travel to distant places. Some do so to capture images of war, poverty, or natural disasters. Many photographers often live in poor conditions while traveling. They want to get as close as possible to the people and situations they are documenting.

Margaret Bourke-White captured this picture of Mahatma Gandhi during one of her trips to India.

Stories in Pictures

Have you ever heard the phrase "a picture is worth a thousand words?" News photos have a special power. They can tell a story in a glance.

What is the difference between a photographer and a photojournalist? A photographer takes pictures. A photojournalist reports the news. That's an important difference.

Life in Pictures

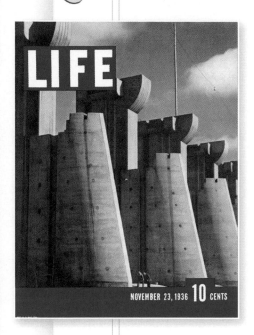

NOVEMBER 23, 1936 10 CENTS

In 1936, Henry Luce (1898–1967) founded *Life* magazine. It was an all-photography weekly newsmagazine. It quickly became popular and sold millions of copies. Some of the most famous news photographs in history appeared in the pages of *Life*, which is now published in short form in some weekly newspapers. The first cover of *Life* magazine (left) featured a photograph of a Montana dam shot by Margaret Bourke-White.

Photojournalists use pictures to tell a story. According to photojournalist Mike Fox, you must "take the time to know what the story is that you are trying to tell." Like reporters, photojournalists must think about who, what, where, when, why, and how. Like reporters, they are always on the go.

The Golden Age

Long ago, drawings were the only pictures in newspapers. Around 1897, a new process made it possible to print photos in newspapers. At the time, cameras were difficult to operate. By 1930, smaller, faster cameras became available. With newly invented flashbulbs, photographers could take pictures at night. Photographs became an important part of the news. The golden age of photojournalism was underway.

World War II ended in 1945. In New York City, thousands of people rushed into the streets to celebrate, including this sailor and nurse. Photojournalist Alfred Eisenstaedt captured the moment in this famous photo.

Photographs tell powerful stories. This woman and child live in a refugee camp in Sudan, Africa.

Technology and Truth

Photojournalists once worried about not having enough film. Now they worry about not having enough battery power. Today's digital cameras can send images around the world in seconds by computer. Cameras have changed, but a photographer's goals remain the same. Photojournalist Susan Brannon says, "The role of a photojournalist is to portray the truth of the events that occur."

Whether they are photojournalists, broadcast journalists, or newspaper reporters — all journalists must report the news quickly and accurately. That means they are writing, interviewing, and shooting on the go!

Career Fact File

JOURNALIST

OUTLOOK

- The United States had about 133,000 journalists in 2006. By 2016, there will be jobs for about 136,000.

- Journalists work for newspapers, magazines, radio and TV stations, and web sites. There are more jobs in larger cities.

WHAT YOU'LL DO

- Journalists collect facts by interviewing people and doing research. They write stories based on those facts.

- Journalists work with editors to change or shorten their stories. Editors decide which stories will go into a newspaper or magazine or be posted on a web site.

- Photojournalists take pictures that will help tell or explain news stories.

- All journalists must work quickly to meet deadlines.

WHAT YOU'LL NEED

- Nearly all journalists must complete four years of college. Some go on for two to three more years to get advanced degrees.

- Broadcast journalists must generally have a distinctive voice and a well-groomed appearance.

WHAT YOU'LL EARN

- Journalists earn from $20,000 to more than $150,000 a year. Those who work in large cities usually earn more. Radio and television work often pays more than print journalism.

Source: U.S. Department of Labor, Bureau of Labor Statistics

GLOSSARY

anchor — on a newscast, the person who reads or introduces the stories

blogs — web logs; web sites usually written by one person that cover news, events, and personal stories

broadcast — to send out news, music, or other programs on radio or television

columnist — a person who writes short essays about the news

deadlines — the dates or times by which articles must be written and submitted to an editor for his or her review

digital — able to be read or used by a computer

editor — in newspapers, a person who checks stories and decides which will be printed; in radio and television, a person who changes stories to make them fit into the available time

editorial — an essay that gives strong opinions about things happening in the news

interpreters — people who can translate one or more foreign languages into another language

interviewed — to have questioned another person to get information

investigated — to have looked into carefully to get facts or information

journalist — a writer or an editor for a news outlet

kicker — the final story on a television news broadcast

lead — the first story on a television news broadcast

producer — in television or radio news, the person who decides which stories will be broadcast and how they fit together

reporters — people who gather information and write about news

technician — a person trained in the special skills of a job

voice-over — a recording of a person's voice that plays while pictures are shown

TO FIND OUT MORE

Books

And the Fans Roared: The Sports Broadcasts That Kept Us on the Edge of Our Seats. Joe Garner, Bob Costas, and George Foreman (Sourcebooks, 2007)

Backstage at a Newscast. Backstage Pass (series). Barbara A. Somervill (Children's Press, 2003)

Muckrakers: How Ida Tarbell, Upton Sinclair, and Lincoln Steffens Helped Expose Scandal, Inspire Reform, and Invent Investigative Journalism. Ann Bausum (National Geographic Society, 2007)

Newspapers. Straight to the Source (series). John Hamilton (Abdo Publishing Company, 2004)

Yellow Journalism. We the People (series). Jason Skog (Compass Point Books, 2007)

Witness to Our Times: My Life as a Photojournalist. Flip Schulke (Cricket Books/Marcato, 2003)

Web Sites

About.com: Journalism
www.journalism.about.com/od/journalismcareers/qt/kids.htm
Ask questions and get answers about careers in journalism.

KidsKhazana
www.kidskhazana.com/blog/archives/category/journalism
Learn more about jobs in journalism.

The Newseum
www.newseum.org
Click on "Take a Video Tour" to visit the news museum.

INDEX

About the Author

William David Thomas lives in Rochester, New York. In his career, Bill has written software documentation, magazine articles, training programs, annual reports, books for children, a few poems, and lots of letters. Bill claims he was once the king of Fiji but gave up the throne to pursue a career as a relief pitcher. It's not true.